INTRODUCTION
to
FERRETS

Owning and caring for these delightful little animals

James McKay

D1427530

No part of this document may be reproduced, stored in a retrievable system or transmitted in any form or by any means electronic, photographic, recording or otherwise, except with the prior written permission of the author and James Wellbeloved.

James McKay hereby asserts and gives notice of his right under Section 77 of the Copyright, Designs and Patents Act, 1988 to be identified as the author of this book.

Text © James E. McKay, 1999. All rights reserved.
Photographs © Jane Burton and James McKay.
Design by Mary Saxe-Falstein

Published by James Wellbeloved
25 Brympton Way
Yeovil, Somerset BA20 2JB

Dedication

To Jane and Thomas for all that you do to support and encourage me.

I would like to thank James Wellbeloved and Co. Ltd. for their help and support in designing and financing the production of this book.

Many thanks must also go to the many friends I have met over the years who never cease to surprise me with the number of questions and amount of support which they put my way.

As always, sincere thanks go to my wife, Jane, and my son, Thomas. Both work untiringly on courses, at displays and behind the scenes to support and help me. Thank you both.

Contents

1. Introduction

2. Choosing your ferret

Where do ferrets come from?
Before you decide to buy
Handling
Taming adult ferrets
Sexing
Putting the sexes together

3. Homes for ferrets

Keeping ferrets indoors
Keeping ferrets outdoors
Cubs
Courts
Positioning
Cleaning
Shavings and bedding

4. Feeding your ferret

A correctly balanced diet
Feeding options which are not recommended
The particular nutritional needs of ferrets
The recommended food for your ferret
Feeding dishes

5. Training your ferret

Playing
Walking on a lead
Car travel
Coming to name
Litter training
Grooming
Ferrets and other pets

6. Shows and Racing

The Ferret Fancy
Fur and size
Condition, eyes and ears
Ferret racing

7. Ferret Ailments

8. First Aid for Ferrets

Appendices

A: Glossary of ferret terms

B: Ferret facts and figures
The adult ferret
Breeding
Pregnancy
Kit development

C: Useful books

D: Useful addresses

E: Rescue and advice centres

1.

INTRODUCTION

To many people, the ferret - and its appeal to millions throughout the world - is a mystery. Even to its ardent fans, this mustelid is still something of a mystery. Where did it come from? How can we ensure proper nutrition of ferrets under our charge? How can vets be persuaded to consider this humble member of the weasel tribe as important as a pedigree dog? These are just some of the questions that this book will help to answer.

I was introduced to ferrets almost by accident, at the tender age of 6 years. I was out with my father when we came across a gamekeeper rabbiting with ferrets, and my father - like most fathers - proceeded to tell me "everything" about ferrets, rabbits and the meaning of life. The 'keeper could not help but overhear, and made his way over to us, having retrieved his ferret from the rabbit burrow. He asked me if I would like to hold the ferret and, without waiting for an answer, thrust the albino animal into my eager arms. My father was furious; he told the 'keeper that all ferrets were killers, and he must remove the animal at once. The 'keeper kept his cool and, taking the ferret from me, opened its mouth and put MY finger in. It didn't bite! From that moment on, I was hooked, and determined to have a ferret of my own, just as soon as possible.

In the 40 years since I had my first encounter with ferrets, I have spent much time studying these animals and their relatives - both in the academic sense and in practical terms. I founded the National Ferret School in 1992, in response to pressure from the many interested people I met on my travels giving displays around the UK, with my Ferret Roadshow. Since then, the family has moved to a 20 acre site, where we have a real school room, many large, spacious courts, and many other items essential to teach everything about ferrets and ferreting. We teach hundreds of people on dozens of courses every year, and now also incorporate lessons on falconry and dogs, since both hawks and dogs are used in ferreting operations.

This book does not seek to be anything other than an introduction to ferrets and their ways, but if it whets your appetite and you want to know more - just contact me at the National Ferret School on telephone 01246-591590 or e-mail me on jamesmckay@honeybank.co.uk

Throughout the book you will find technical terms. Please refer to Appendix A and B on ferret terms, facts and figures later in the book where they are explained in detail.

Albino ferret kits
just out of the nest

Nesting in straw

2.

CHOOSING YOUR FERRET

Where do ferrets come from?

Before you decide to buy

Handling

Taming adult ferrets

Sexing

Putting the sexes together

Fitchet with
distinctive mask

Where do ferrets come from?

Where did the first ferret originate? No-one really knows but today many people, including myself, are of the opinion that the ferret we know today is a domesticated European polecat (Mustela putorius). Ferrets are inter-fertile with polecats, and so all offspring are viable (can produce young of their own). Even the accepted scientific name of the domesticated ferret (Mustela putorius furo) indicates that many scientists hold the same view.

Ferrets are mentioned in the Old Testament of the Holy Bible (in the book of Leviticus), but this cannot be the same animal, although some tribes in the area do use a mustelid to hunt subterranean animals in the same way that we use ferrets against rabbits. In the UK and some other countries, ferrets have traditionally been kept for using to control rabbits and rats, and this tradition continues.

Today's ferrets are likely to be kept as pets, although there are still many people who work them on rabbits and rats. Ferrets have also been used for threading cables through pipes and conduits, the sport of ferret racing, and are fast becoming a very popular "fancy" (exhibition) animal.

Above all, ferrets are fun! They love playing, respond to their owner's voice and are full of mischief. They combine many of the advantages of a dog or cat, with very few of their disadvantages, and have ousted many other small pets from the popularity stakes in many western countries.

Scientific classification

The ferret belongs to the weasel tribe, or mustelidae ("seeker of mice", the name refers to the musty smell), and is related to such animals as the otter, badger and the skunk. It is also a carnivore, and thus related to cats, dogs and civets.

The mustelidae are to be found all over the world, in every continent except Australia and Antarctica and their habitat ranges from arctic tundra to tropical rainforest, on land, in trees, in rivers and in the ocean.

Before you decide to buy

Before buying a ferret - or any other animal for that matter - you should think long and hard. Ferrets live for up to 14 years, and will require attention for every day of their lives. They will need feeding, cleaning and even veterinary attention. All of this costs time and money - sometimes more than one had bargained for. You should carefully consider the implications on your lifestyle, and ensure that you can supply all of the ferret's needs for its entire life.

Having said that, I feel that the pleasure and sheer fun that ferrets can give to their owners far outweighs the work and effort needed, and I can heartily recommend them to those willing to make the effort to give them all they will need.

Having decided that you really do want to keep one or more ferrets, you should start to look at what is on offer. Obviously, a suitable cage and supply of suitable food should be ready before you make your purchase (see later chapters in this book for more details), as should a good supply of shavings and bedding.

The ferret's colour is, to some people, very important. If you are buying your ferret with a view to breeding show winning stock, it is essential that you buy top quality stock of the correct variety (colour) and standard. If you are buying a ferret for a pet or as a working animal, colour is not important; simply buy the ferret that meets your other selection criteria and appeals to you.

Handling

There is absolutely no purpose in having an animal that one is fearful of handling, since this will mean that the animal is not handled at all, and neither will the cage be cleaned as often as it should be. This creates an imprisoned animal, which will be aggressive through fear; it is cruelty to the ferret. Well-bred and well-handled ferrets are as unlikely to bite as dogs or cats of similar backgrounds.

No ferret can ever be too "quiet" (tame); even ferrets used for hunting need to be just as manageable as pet ferrets. After all, if you cannot handle a ferret in normal conditions, how will you fare when the ferret has had a fight with a rabbit or a rat, or is simply excited at the action? By regular, considerate handling, even the most "aggressive" ferret will soon calm down, although with older ferrets, this will take more effort on your part than would a young kit. We believe that there is no such thing as a bad ferret, simply too many bad owners of ferrets.

Initial handling

It is best for all concerned that handling should begin as early as possible; if you have bred a litter from your jill, the kits should be handled regularly from the time that their eyes are open, and they are wandering around their cage. If the jill has been handled properly, and is truly tame, she will not usually object to this. This is how we treat our ferrets. We have a rule at the National Ferret School that every ferret must be handled every day of its life. Thus we can - with the utmost confidence - allow anyone to handle our ferrets without any fear of bites.

Begin by gently stroking the kits, at the same time talking in low, soothing tones. After only a very short time, they will accept, and even welcome, this attention. After a couple of days of this, pick up the kits (one at a time) by placing one hand around its chest, and the other under its back end. This will help ensure that the animal's weight is evenly distributed, and no undue pressures are exerted on the quite fragile body.

Having established an acceptance of your handling the kits, the next step is to get them to accept that your fingers are wonderful - but definitely not on the menu! To do this, mix a couple of raw eggs with some full cream milk; assuming that you are right handed, dip the fingers of your left hand into the mix, and offer them to the kits. The young ferrets will be attracted by the smell and will start licking your fingers. Some will become very excited, and may nip your flesh; at this age, the sensation is only mildly uncomfortable. However, you must not allow them to get away with this action, as they will think it is acceptable behaviour. Instead, as a kit nibbles your finger, gently flick him on the side of his face; this should be more of a shock to the kit, than actual pain. He will probably hesitate, and then recommence his nibbling; flick him again. After a few days of this treatment, none of the kits will even dream of biting your finger. Hence, when the animals are strong enough to hurt you, they will have no desire to.

Taming adult ferrets

With adult ferrets, the procedure is very similar, in that we are going to train them that certain actions are unacceptable. With rescued ferrets, which are very frightened, picking up may be quite difficult. The best way to achieve this is either with a gloved hand (a method that we never use, as a glove always deadens sensation, and makes holding a ferret difficult and uncomfortable for both handler and ferret), or by first pulling the animal firmly but slowly backwards by the tail. This will make the ferret automatically dig in his front feet, and try to put his weight to the front. As he does this, take hold of his torso (keeping hold of his tail) with the other hand, placing the thumb and little fingers around the ferret's chest, under his arms. Keep the other three fingers behind his head. This is the best way I have ever found of securely and safely holding a struggling adult ferret. To calm a ferret - of any age - hold him around his torso, and gently swing him backwards and forwards, gently pulling his body through the half closed fist of the other hand. This stroking is something that all ferrets seem to enjoy, and it always calms them.

To teach an adult ferret not to bite takes a little more time and patience than it does for a kit. Holding him as previously described, offer the knuckles of your other hand; it is important that it is the knuckles and no other part of the hand, as there should be no loose flesh for him to grab hold of (bite). As he tries to bite you, quickly move your hand away, and gently slap or flick him on the side of the face; as with the kits, your intention should be to shock him rather than inflict physical pain.

Immediately after the slap, swing him again, as previously described. After a few minutes of swinging, offer him your knuckles again. As he tries to bite, slap him again. Repeat this process for about 10-15 minutes two or three times every day and, after a few days, you should have a tame ferret who is a pleasure to handle.

Sexing

The sexing of ferrets - even as very young kits - is simplicity itself. As in most mammals, this is achieved by examining the distance between the anus and the genitals. If the distance is short, it is a female; if the distance is greater, it is a male.

In adults, the differences are quite marked and in summer un-neutered hobs will have obvious testicles. There is also a difference in the size and overall shape of the animals. The hob is almost twice the size of the jill, and the hob's head is very broad, while the jill's is long and slender. These differences in size and shape are known as "sexual dimorphism" and are a very easy way to tell the sexes of adult ferrets.

Fitchet hob and jill pair grooming each other
(allogrooming) during courtship.

Putting the sexes together

The sex and numbers of ferrets to be kept are yet more considerations for the new purchaser, and ones to which much thought should be given. Most people (myself included) feel that ferrets are best kept not singly but in groups. I have to say, though, that the polecat (the ferret's ancestor) is a solitary animal, and I know of many people who keep a single ferret, and all seems well. If you decide that you wish to keep more than one ferret, you should choose the group make-up very carefully.

Two hobs, once they have reached sexual maturity (in the first spring after their birth) are likely to fight, inflicting quite horrific wounds on each other); this is even likely to happen where the hobs are siblings. A hob and a jill kept together will lead to litters, which you may not always want. Jills kept on their own will probably live quite happily without fighting. However, jills have other problems.

Female fitchet kit, five weeks old

In the first spring after they are born, jills will come into oestrus. In common with many other animals - including chickens and horses - the ferret's oestrus is regulated by photoperiodism. In other words, she will come on heat when the days get longer, and the nights shorter, ie in the spring. Unless taken out of season - either by injection of hormones or by mating - she will remain in season throughout the summer months.

If a jill is not mated immediately that she is on heat, the levels of oestrogen (the female sex hormone) will build up, causing progressive depression of the bone marrow. This can result in a condition known as pancytopenia - the abnormal depression of all three cell types of the blood - a condition that is potentially fatal. In other words, if a jill is left in oestrus (on heat) for any length of time, she will almost inevitably die before reaching her full life expectancy.

We recommend that any ferret kept purely as a pet, and with no intention of breeding, should be neutered, i.e. males castrated or jills spayed. By carrying out this action, the pet owner reduces the problems associated with the keeping of ferrets of either sex, and it is possible for several neutered ferrets - regardless of sex - to live happily in the same cage. Neutering will also reduce the smell of the ferrets, again of both sexes.

However, if it is desirable to keep all options open, the best method of removing the risk of serious health problems linked to prolonged oestrogenic exposure is to have the jill mated with a vasectomised male ferret (a hoblet), or given a "jill-jab" by a vet. Where large numbers of jills are kept, then the ferret owner really cannot afford not to have at least one hoblet.

A hoblet will be able to take jills out of oestrus for about 7 - 8 years, thereby repaying the investment made by having him vasectomised several times over. Savings will be made on food, time and trouble that kits would cause the owner and, of course, there will be fewer unwanted ferrets to be abandoned by unscrupulous people.

A jill mated with a hoblet will usually have a pseudo-pregnancy (phantom pregnancy) following the mating. This may result in the jill's stomach swelling, she may produce milk, and may nest build. In other words, she will exhibit all of the symptoms of being pregnant, with one major difference - at the end of the 42 day "pregnancy", she will not produce a litter

The jill will, however, come back into oestrus about 3 - 4 weeks after the end of the pseudo-pregnancy, when she will require mating again. By the end of the second "pregnancy", the summer will be almost over, and the jill will not come on heat again until the following spring.

Many ferret clubs recommend and even encourage owners of hoblets to lend them to owners of jills in heat, but this practice is irresponsible, and fraught with dangers. The risk of the spread of diseases such as Aleutian disease, distemper, enteritis and influenza is far too great. Encouraging the loan of hoblets simply dissuades people from making the investment for themselves, and is not a sign of responsible animal ownership.

If owners do not wish to invest in a hoblet of their own, or have only a small number of jills, "jill jabs" - injections with drugs such as proligestone (Delvosteron ®) - are often a viable alternative which allows owners to keep their options open, without endangering their ferrets or producing unwanted litters. One of the few side effects of hormone injections is temporary hair loss at the injection site.

Fitchet kits,
a hob and a jill,
both just five weeks old.

Although a jill comes into season early in the spring, and will remain so until she is removed from season by a mating or hormone injection, the obvious signs of her condition will not always be present. When she first comes into season, her vulva will swell noticeably, often protruding from her body by over a centimetre. Within 7 - 10 days of mating, this swelling will reduce, but it will also reduce (albeit temporarily) after a couple of weeks even if she is not mated. This does not, however, mean that she is not in season as, in the next few weeks, her vulva will again swell to very large proportions.

To sum up, we at the National Ferret School recommend serious ferret owners, who may well wish to have one or more litters out of their jills, to keep two jills and one hoblet. This keeps all options open and, at a later date, the ferret keeper is able to either buy-in a hob or borrow the stud services of a suitable hob to cover one or both of the jills.

Jill fitchet in her summer coat
and hob fitchet still in his winter coat.

3.

HOMES FOR FERRETS

Keeping ferrets indoors

Keeping ferrets outdoors

Cubs

Courts

Positioning

Cleaning

Shavings and bedding

In the UK, it is the rule rather than the exception to keep ferrets in outside cages, although it must be said that more and more people in Britain are now keeping ferrets as household pets. This is the first major decision that you should take, once you have decided to become a ferret owner, and before you purchase any animal. For animals kept in captivity, their cage is all too often, quite literally, their world. For this reason, owners must ensure that an animal's cage fulfils all of its roles adequately, thus ensuring the ferret's welfare and well-being. If a ferret is to live its full 14 years, its cage must be 100% suit-able as its home. To generalise, in the UK there are two main types of ferret keepers - those who see their animals as pets, and those who see them as working animals. Pet keepers tend to keep their animals indoors, while the keepers of workers tend to keep their charges outside the home.

Keeping ferrets indoors

If you decide to keep your ferret inside, then your choice of cage will probably be limited to one of the many sold at pet stores throughout the country, and designed as homes for "house ferrets" or similar sized animals. These cages differ from outside cages in that they do not provide much shelter from the elements; as they are not intended to be outside, they don't need to.

Indoor cages need not be too big, as many house ferrets are allowed the freedom of the human home, while the family is there, but confined to their cage at other times, when they cannot be adequately supervised. However, it should be noted that ferrets have a penchant for getting into the places that you really don't want them to. Washing machines, pantries and even knicker drawers are some of the places I have heard of these animals invading! Other household pets - hamsters, mice etc - may also be put at risk by the ferret's freedom.

If your ferrets are to be allowed total free access to all parts of the human home, you must take precautions to prevent their injury. These precautions include informing all visitors that ferrets are loose in the home (this protects both ferrets and humans!), and ensuring that all cupboards, drawers etc are kept closed. It is advisable to keep all outside doors and windows closed too, as these can act has avenues of escape for the ferrets, and may allow access for cats or other potential predators of your ferrets such as foxes or badgers.

Keeping ferrets outdoors

The ferret living outside should be kept in a large hutch, or cub, as it is correctly called. Even better is a large aviary-type cage, known as a court. This is the traditional method of keeping ferrets, and has much to commend it. At the National Ferret School, we keep our ferrets in courts throughout the winter, but in the summer, the hobs and breeding jills are all housed in separate cubs containing just the one animal.

Obviously, ferrets living out-of-doors must be supplied with a fully weatherproof cage, which is big enough, and of the correct dimensions, to allow the ferrets to indulge in their natural behaviour. It may come as a surprise to some, but ferrets love to climb and, if given the opportunity, will spend a great deal of their time doing just this.

Cubs

Cubs are simply well-built hutches, similar to the type that many rabbits are kept in. The minimum size for a cub suitable for two ferrets is 1.5m x 0.75m x 0.75m (approximately 5ft. wide x 2'6" deep x 2'6" high). It is better to err on the large size than give animals cramped quarters. A nest box must also be supplied for sleeping quarters. This can be fixed to the outside of the cub, thus giving more space for the ferrets to live, or may form an integral part of the cub. Access to the nest box should be through a small "pop-hole", measuring about 5 cm in diameter for jills, and 7 - 10 cm diameter for hobs.

Raise the cub off the floor, by adding legs; this will help reduce temperature loss by cold striking up from the cold, damp ground, and also put the cub at a convenient height for you to work on, when cleaning and performing other maintenance duties. Rather than waste the space below the cub, it is possible to turn it into an exercise area for the ferrets. This is easily achieved by covering the back and both sides with weld mesh, and putting a pair of opening doors on the front; the addition of a solid timber floor will complete the exercise area. The ferrets can gain access to this exercise area via a length of corrugated piping, such as that sold for draining soil. By providing a shutter which can seal off the access, along with a separate nest box that can be placed in the bottom area, you will also have made a separate cub, for emergency use, or to separate ferrets in the breeding season.

Courts

If you have the space, then ferret courts are much better - for both the ferrets and yourself - than cubs. Our courts consist of a timber frame (50 mm x 50 mm), covered with 5-gauge welded mesh. They vary in size from 4m x 4m to 2m x 1.5m, but all are 2m high. (That's about 13' x 13' to 6'6" x 5' and 6'6" high.) This height is as much for convenience to the keepers, as it is a design consideration for the ferrets; at this height, a human adult can easily stand and work in the court, without having to adopt a very uncomfortable crouching position, helping facilitate cleaning and maintenance. However, as stated earlier, ferrets, although not as agile as their cousins the martens, do like to climb; the extra height means that the court can be furnished with branches for them to enjoy this activity, thus increasing their living space. All of our courts have sloping concrete floors, for ease of cleaning.

Nest boxes may be placed inside the courts, or affixed to the outside. Placing nest boxes at different heights within each court, will give the ferrets more choice, and is extremely beneficial, but NOT if the court is to be used for breeding purposes, as the kits could fall and injure themselves.

Albino kits

Although ferrets enjoy fresh air, and both a little sunshine and rain, it is essential that they also have access to shelter from these two elements, without having to seek refuge in their nest boxes.

Positioning

The correct positioning of your ferret cub or court is of paramount importance, and should obviously be considered before construction of the cage begins. Ideally, the chosen site should give protection from excesses of wind, rain, sun, heat and cold. In particular, you should avoid placing any type of cage in direct sunlight, as ferrets quickly succumb to heat exhaustion, which is often fatal.

Cleaning

Ferrets are extremely clean animals, spending much time on their own personal hygiene, and are very particular where they empty their bladders and bowels. The latrine area chosen by ferrets is almost always in a corner, or at least against a vertical edge, and as far away from their sleeping quarters as possible. This habit makes life easy for the ferret keeper, since part of the daily routine should be to shovel and scrape out the area of the latrine(s), thus reducing the build up of faeces, and thus smell and the risk of disease.

Placing a washing up type plastic bowl in the appropriate corner will make life even easier. Cut two sides down to about 2-3 cm high, and fill with soil, sand or shavings. Place the bowl in the corner with the high sides against the walls of the cage. By keeping ready a second, identical bowl the cage can be kept very clean. Simply remove the soiled bowl and replace it immediately with the fresh one. Clean out and replenish the soiled bowl, and repeat this process every day, rotating the bowls.

To ensure that harmful bacteria are not allowed to build up, causing potential medical problems for the ferrets, a top quality disinfectant must be used, once all of the solid matter has been removed from the cage. Under no circumstances should any phenolic disinfectant be used, as this is potentially lethal to ferrets (and, incidentally, cats). Phenolic disinfectants turn white when added to water, and so are easily identified.

Use a surface active disinfectant, such as Trigene or Dettox. Used as per the manufacturer's instructions, these are perfectly safe for ferrets. All cleaning utensils, dishes and bottles should also be periodically cleaned in one of these disinfectants, ensuring that all traces are rinsed from food and water utensils before they are returned to the ferrets' cage.

Shavings and bedding

Never use sawdust in a ferret's cage, as this may cause breathing and eye problems. Wood shavings are ideal for lining the floor, as they soak up moisture and faeces very easily. They are also easy and cheap to obtain and dispose of. The best method of disposal of soiled bedding and shavings is to burn the material. Make sure this is carried out well away from both ferret and human homes.

For bedding, in outside cubs and courts, top quality straw should be used. Hay, although softer and seemingly better (to humans) can cause problems to the ferrets due to the seeds contained in the ears of the hay. Never use any straw which smells musty, or seems excessively dusty. Indoor ferrets can be bedded down on shredded paper or even old sweaters, T-shirts etc, and these should be disposed of when soiled.

Albino kits
curled up in straw

FEEDING YOUR FERRET

A correctly balanced diet

Feeding options which are not recommended

The particular nutritional needs of ferrets

The recommended food for your ferret

Feeding dishes

Fitchet kits
just 5 weeks old

It is important that your give your ferrets all the care and attention which they need. Looked after properly, your ferrets could live to be more than 14 years. Good husbandry, coupled with the feeding of a top quality balanced diet will help them achieve their full life expectancy.

The correct diet - balanced to give the right amounts of the relevant constituents - is essential for a long and healthy life for your ferrets, and is easily attainable. It is also good for you, as it will mean less hassle and fewer vets' bills! Ferrets fed the proper diet will lead longer, happier and healthier lives, and repay the investment many times.

There is an old saying - "You are what you eat" - and this applies to ferrets. A good diet for ferrets must be healthy for them, affordable for you, and readily available. Fed a proper diet, the ferret's faeces will be very dark, solid and have little smell; when fed a poor diet, the faeces are soft and often semi-liquid, very pale in colour, and extremely smelly; in human terms, it is rather like living with perpetual diarrhoea - not a pleasant prospect! In addition, the ferret will lead a very unhealthy and short life.

A CORRECTLY BALANCED DIET

All animals require certain items in their diet, with quite large differences between species. All animals require water, fat, carbohydrate, protein, fibre, some minerals and some vitamins. It is necessary to have a basic under-standing of what each does.

Protein

Proteins, or amino acids, are essential for growth and tissue maintenance, and should form about 35-40% of the ferrets' diet. Proteins are present in meats, eggs and milk. While all ferrets require a high protein diet, this is even more important when considering nursing mothers, their kits and young ferrets in general. Likewise, males used for stud also require a higher protein content in their diet.

Carbohydrates

Carbohydrates provide the body with heat and material for growth, excess amounts being stored as fat in the body, often leading to obesity. As everyone knows, this can cause medical problems and difficulties in the ferrets' breeding; a fat, overweight ferret will not be as active, nor as agile as he should be, and so will not be as happy.

Fats

Fats are the richest source of energy that can be fed, giving about 2fi times the calories, weight for weight, that carbohydrates do. Obviously, feeding too much fat to your ferret will lead to an obese - and therefore unhealthy - ferret. Both fats and carbohydrates, however, do have a place in your ferret's diet, particularly when the animal is very active, and also in winter. During cold weather, the ferret's body breaks down fats and carbohydrates to keep the body warm. Ferrets, along with many other types of animal, will put down more fat at the onset of winter. This is not harmful, rather it would be harmful to prevent your ferret from doing this.

Vitamins

Vitamins are chemical compounds, essential for growth, health, normal metabolism, and general physical well-being. There are two main types of vitamin - water-soluble and fat-soluble. Water-soluble vitamins cannot be stored in the body, and so the day's food must contain the day's requirements of these vitamins. Fat-soluble vitamins can be stored in the body and, if too many are taken in at one time, they can be stored for use when the body needs them. However, an excess of such vitamins may cause toxic levels to accumulate in storage areas such as the liver. It is important to remember that an excess of any fat-soluble vitamin can lead to long term physical problems. You should also remember that a lack of essential vitamins can be detrimental to the ferret's health.

FEEDING OPTIONS WHICH ARE NOT RECOMMENDED

Ferrets are obligate carnivores, a word derived from the Latin carnis, meaning flesh, and vorare, to devour. As such, their natural diet is one of flesh, ie. whole carcasses of mammals, birds, reptiles, fish, amphibia and even some invertebrates. Many people object to feeding such items (which can, of course, only be fed dead), and it has to be said that a ferret fed on such a diet, although healthy, will have a very strong odour and may not be getting a fully balanced diet. To many, this kind of diet is impossible to supply. Do not despair! There are acceptable alternatives.

Bread and milk.

Many old-time ferret keepers fed their animals on a diet of milk sops (bread and milk). This is not recommended, as ferrets fed on such a diet will have constant diarrhoea, making them very smelly. Such a poor diet will also have serious long-term repercussions on the health of the ferret.

Day-old chicks.

Do not feed day old cockerels (chicks) to your ferrets. These are widely available, and very cheap. However, there are great risks to ferrets fed on a diet in which day-olds feature greatly. Research indicates that day-old chicks are very low in calcium, protein and fat, and contain very little vitamin E. The feeding of day-old chicks has also been shown to cause such problems as hypocalcaemia, actinomycosis (a thickening and swelling of the neck), osteodystrophy, thiamine deficiency, posterior paralysis (the "staggers"), and other maladies. Quite apart from all this, day-old chicks attract flies and can rapidly go bad, causing stomach upsets. New evidence also suggests that the egg white found in chicks can cause bald patches in ferrets' coats.

Canned dog food and cat food.

A ready supply of quality meat is always available from supermarkets, in the shape of tinned dog and cat food, and many ferreters use this as a basis for their ferrets' diet. However, these are obviously not designed for ferrets, and many will need to have vitamin and mineral supplements added to them, before they can be fed.

"Pet meat".

Many pet shops now sell 'pet meat' or brawn, of different flavours, and some of these brands can be fed, but again, many will require supplementing. At the very least, all tinned dog and cat foods (and other similar foods) must be supplemented with the addition of bonemeal powder. This will ensure that the ferrets receive adequate amounts of calcium, vital to the well-being of the ferrets and essential for the animal to grow strong bones and teeth - plus multi-vitamins, or a combined mineral and vitamin supplement, such as SA 37, which is available from pet shops and veterinary surgeons.

Dry dog food and cat food.

Over the years, ferret owners have tried many of the complete diets intended for cats or dogs, on their ferrets, often with some success. However, these diets are not intended or designed for ferrets, and will obviously have nutritional deficiencies for the species, unless supplemented. In particular, it is doubtful if any dog or cat foods will have a high enough protein content, or the correct doses of the relevant vitamins and minerals etc.

THE PARTICULAR NUTRITIONAL NEEDS OF FERRETS

Ferrets simply have different nutritional requirements from either dogs or cats. They have higher energy needs and a shorter digestive tract than cats or dogs and being carnivores, their primary protein source must be meat. This means that they derive little benefit from the corn and soya protein sources found in many cat and dog foods because ferrets' digestions are relatively inefficient at absorbing vegetable proteins.

Remember, you should do everything in your power to ensure that your ferrets lead long, healthy lives; feeding a suitable diet is one of the best ways to achieve this. Ferrets fed a proper diet will be active and healthy, requiring fewer visits to the vet, and giving you more enjoyment.

The recommended diet for your ferret

Some years ago, we at the National Ferret School began trialling a new, complete and balanced dry food made specially for ferrets. Produced by James Wellbeloved & Co Ltd, it is sold under the name of "Ferret Complete", and, after trialling the diet for some considerable time, we can recommend it highly. In fact we now do not feed our ferrets any other food than "Ferret Complete".

Feeding a complete diet such as this will ensure good nutrition, reduce the smell of the ferret, reduce the amount and smell of faeces produced, and is easy for you to obtain and store.

If your ferret won't eat this complete diet, try moistening it slightly, with warm water. This increases the palatability in the same way that heating a sausage roll does for us. Once your ferret is eating the diet, reduce and then cut out the water on the food, always ensuring that you give your pet a constant supply of clean, fresh water at all times.

Feeding dishes

If you accept our recommendation and feed Ferret Complete, you will need to give the food in a dish. Use heavy ceramic dishes, as these will not be tipped over by the exuberance of the ferrets in the cage. Never use galvanised dishes, as ferrets will quickly succumb to zinc toxicity.

If your ferret develops the annoying habit of scraping all of the food of the dish, wasting the food and spreading it everywhere, try using a spaniel dish. These are intended to prevent a spaniel's ears from falling in its food, and taper to the top. Your ferret will not be able to empty the dish now!

Water is best provided in a gravity-feed bottle of the type sold in pet shops for small animals. Keep it clean and regularly topped up, changing the water at least twice a week, and daily in warm weather.

Two and a half weeks old
kit yawning

Jill ferret in ferns

5.

TRAINING YOUR FERRET

Playing

Walking on a lead

Car travel

Coming to name

Litter training

Grooming

Ferrets and other pets

6-week-old fitchet kit
playing with catnip mouse

It is surprising just what "tricks" you can teach a ferret, given time, patience and a little insight into the ferret's language. A ferret obviously does not speak as we know speech, but it does make noises and says even more with its body language. You may wonder why anyone should be interested in learning ferret language, but the reason is obvious - if you are to teach him, you must be able to communicate, and communication is best when it is two-way.

When a ferret is angry or frightened, it will make its hair stand on end, looking rather like a toilet brush. At the same time, it will hiss and spit; if really angry, it will release a foul smelling fluid from its back end. Such a ferret needs treating with the utmost respect! Try to work out just what is frightening him. Has he suddenly seen you, startling himself? Have you accidentally trodden on his paw? Is there a strange dog or cat in the area? Any of these things may upset the ferret.

When your ferret is upset, calm him by talking in a soothing voice; don't try to pick him up until you are sure he realises who you are, and that you are not going to hurt him. Even the nicest of ferrets will react by biting if they are frightened or upset.

Playing

When a ferret wants to play, he will tell you by his body language, and his voice. I always think that a ferret in a playful mood resembles Tigger, from Winnie the Pooh. The ferret will arch its back and bounce around holding all four legs stiffly. At the same time, it will move its head from side to side, often with its mouth opening and shutting. The whole time the ferret is doing this, it will be chattering in a very happy manner. If the ferret is out of its cage, for instance on the lawn, it will chase you or other humans in the area, trying to get them to play. Often ferrets will chase the family dog or cat.

When first seen, many owners believe that the ferret has gone mad, and is intent on attacking them; it merely wants to play!

Ferrets do play rough; they use their teeth to grab hold of their playmate and will often pounce from atop stones, bales of straw or any other vantage point in the area. I find my ferrets love being flicked up and away just off the ground, always provided that their landing spot will not be a hard material, such as concrete.

Table tennis balls make excellent toys for ferrets, as do the type of ball with which golfers practice their sport. It is possible to buy large, hollow balls into which the ferret can climb, or even a series of tunnels which clip together. Personally, I give our ferrets lengths of pipe used for underground drains, and plastic plant pots to play in. Use you imagination, and save money while still giving your ferrets lots of fun.

Walking on a lead

Many people take their ferrets for a walk and, as with dogs, they attach a lead to the animal for safety's sake. As with dogs, ferrets will not take to the lead instantly, and it is worth spending a few moments to get the ferret accustomed to the harness (much better than a collar) and lead before starting the actual walk.

The harness for the ferret should be soft but strong, is usually made from either leather or nylon, and must be a secure fit. Ferrets are extremely supple and can easily wriggle out of a collar or harness that is not tight enough; if the collar/harness is too tight, however, the ferret could be asphyxiated. I do not like the harnesses made from one piece of nylon or leather, but prefer the ones consisting of two collars - one of which goes around the ferret's neck, and the other behind its front legs. Both collars are joined together by a third piece of material, which goes down between the shoulder blades. On to this third piece of the harness is fitted a D ring, to which the lead is attached.

Every harness I have bought for my ferrets has required new holes for secure fastening, and I find a special leather hole punch to be an indispensable aid for this operation. While securely holding the ferret, place the harness around his neck and, with a felt-tip pen, mark the place where the hole needs to be. Once you have punched the hole, you can try the harness on the ferret. Ensure that it is tight enough not to come over the animal's head, while not being so tight

that the ferret cannot breathe. Next fasten the back strap, which should be placed behind the ferret's front legs; this strap does not have to be quite as snug a fit as the neck one. Once the harness has been fitted, place the ferret on the floor; he will immediately try his hardest to get the harness off, and so he should be distracted for 5-10 minutes, by which time he will have forgotten it, and will thus accept it.

When this has happened - and not before - it is time to attach the lead. Again, the ferret will react to the new encumbrance and so requires distracting until such time as it is accepted. Once this is achieved, you are ready to embark on your first walk together. For the first few walks, and always when you are taking your ferret into a public place, use a short (about 1 metre) lead. Only when your ferret is totally happy on his walkies - and even then only in the safety of your garden, should you use a longer lead.

Don't be too ambitious; a 30-mile route march will not be a happy event for the ferret! The first few walks should be taken at a very leisurely pace, and not cover more than a few hundred metres. The ferret will keep stopping at every new smell and sight, and you may well have to drag him from some of them. Try to make the whole experience of the outing a pleasurable one, for both of you. Be patient and remember that the things which you take for granted, and to which you react in a blasé manner, will be entirely new and mysterious - maybe even frightening - to your ferret.

Be extremely cautious of dogs - however well you may think that you know them; it is all too common for ferrets on "walkies" to be attacked and injured - or even killed - by dogs. It is also vital that all ferrets taken to areas frequented by dogs, eg public paths, parks etc, are vaccinated against canine distemper - one of the biggest killers of ferrets.

Car travel

For travelling in a vehicle, your ferret should be placed in the security and comfort of a pet carrier, sold in pet shops for the transport of cats and other small animals. Line the bottom of the carrier with newspaper, and place an old towel or some soft straw on top of this. Don't give any water or food while travelling, but make sure that you take some with you, along with a dish for the food and a dish or bottle for the water.

While in the car, make sure that the carrier is not left in the sun; always remember that the sun's position relative to the car will change as the car is driven along! If you are travelling a long distance, make sure that when you stop for refreshments and a stretch, the ferret is also accorded this privilege; ferrets dehydrate very quickly, and so it is essential that they are offered water every couple of hours.

Coming to name

It is quite possible - and relatively straightforward - to teach your ferret to come to you when called. This is achieved in exactly the same manner that a dog and any other animal is trained - by association of ideas. Quite simply, you need to get your ferret to associate a sound or word with something dear to its heart. In the first instance, this is best done by getting your ferret to associate its name with food, or rather a very tasty treat or tit-bit.

Although it is simplest to start from the day you acquire your ferret, it is still possible to teach an old ferret new tricks - it just takes more patience and more time. Make a noise - or speak a short word - when you put your ferret's food in its dish, or as suggested earlier, to give the ferret a tasty treat. Within a couple of days, the ferret will come straight out of its nest to the sound, and run to the front of the cage to get its food. Next, leave out the food, but make the call as usual. This time, when the ferret comes to you, pick it up and give it a nice cuddle. Your ferret will be just as pleased to receive its cuddle, as it would be its food and - Hey Presto - your ferret is trained to come to call! You can, if you wish, give the ferret its food or treat at the end of the cuddle session, but this is not essential.

Litter training

Ferrets are very clean animals and fastidious about their toilet arrangements. Even without any training, your ferret will always use the same place in its cage as a toilet, both for defecation and urination. This is usually the corner of the cage furthest from the nesting area. Problems occur, of course, when your ferret is given the run of the family (i.e. human) home. You don't want the ferret messing on the carpet, or against the suite.

Start by giving your ferret a proper little loo. This is easily made from a plastic washing-up bowl. Ferrets like to put their bottom in the air when defecating or urinating, and so we can re-model the bowl to suit our purposes. Cut two sides of the bowl down to about 3cm from the bottom; these sides will face outwards when the bowl is in position. Put a sheet of newspaper in the bottom of the bowl, and then cover it with about 1fi cm of shavings, sand or soil. Clear out the corner of the cage currently used by the ferrets, saving a little of the soiled shavings; these should be placed in the bowl, in the high corner. Place the bowl in the selected corner, with the high sides against the side of the cage. The next time your ferret uses the loo, he will go into the bowl. By making two of these bowls for each ferret cage, you have will always have a fresh one to put in place of a soiled one, while the dirty one is thoroughly cleaned.

When your ferret is given its liberty around the family home, put one of these bowls in the room in which the ferret is allowed to run around. Always place the bowl in the same place, and in the early days, ensure there is a small amount of faeces in the bowl. After a few uses, your ferret will know where to find his loo, and always use it.

Grooming

All ferrets will benefit from grooming; indeed many get to love the felling of being pampered in exactly the same way that humans like the idea. Use a fine-toothed comb and a soft brush, and gently groom your pet from nose to tail, making sure that you are very gentle, and stopping if your ferret shows any signs of being uncomfortable.

This grooming will help keep your ferret's coat in perfect condition, while also giving you the opportunity to check him over for any injuries, cuts, bites, skin problems or ectoparasites.

Ferrets & other pets

Ferrets are capable of getting along fine with cats and dogs, but don't let him near small rodents or rabbits. He will probably invite them to dinner - with them on the menu! Introduce your pets carefully, preferably on neutral ground and after both have been fed. Put both on leads, as this will give you more control, should anything start to go awry. It is important that you can under-stand the body language of both pets, since this will tell you how things are going, and give you prior warning of any attack.

Once the two animals will accept each other while on their leads, take one off, and try them, keeping a watchful eye on both parties. If this goes well, then it is time to let both off their leads, while still keeping a very watchful eye on them. No matter how well you believe your pets to get on together, never leave them free in the same room with no supervision.

Fitchets curled up together

6.

FERRET SHOWS AND RACING

The Ferret Fancy

Fur and size

Condition, eyes and ears

Ferret racing

To many people, having a pet ferret is not enough; they want to compete with their pet. In the case of ferrets, there are two area in which competitions are held - ferret shows and ferret racing.

The ferret fancy

Ferret shows are held all over the country, throughout the year, but mainly during the summer months. At these shows, ferrets from far and wide, of all sizes and shapes, both young and old, male and female, are judged against standards. These standards describe the organising club's idea of the perfect ferret; some are written down, others exist only in the minds of the judges, and so vary enormously between countries, regions, clubs and even individuals. If you want to be successful at showing, you need to carefully study the standards for your area, and your animals must comply with them if you are to stand a chance of winning.

Obviously, then, it is impossible to list the exact standards under which your ferret will be judged, but the following will give you a guide. The categories under which points are allotted are usually;

> Colour and markings
> Type
> Fur
> Size
> Condition
> Eyes and ears

Colour and markings

Patterned varieties will receive 50% of the points for this category for colour and markings and 50% points for pattern. At some shows, different colours are judged in separate classes, while at other shows, all varieties are judged together, often separated by sex or age. Whichever method is used, the overall results should come from the result of the comparison of each animal against its standard, and NOT each other.

Type

"Type", or configuration as it is sometimes called, refers to the overall shape of the ferret. The ferret should have a long, lean body, which arches when the animal is at rest, with short legs; its gait should be easy and effortless. The tail should be about half as long as the body. The head should be proportionate to the body, with the hob having a much broader skull; the face of the animal may be pointed or blunt, as neither is detrimental to the animal. The head should be well set into the body, the profile showing a smooth curve from nose over head, to nape of neck. The neck should be cylindrical, and noticeably long, blending gradually with the slender and elongated thorax and abdomen.

Fur and size

The fur should be soft and very dense, with due allowances made for animals which have been neutered, as this tends to give them a better coat. The coat should consist of fine under-fur and longer, more coarse guard hairs, and the tail should be well furred.

The ferret should be lean, and well muscled but not fat, and of a size which would allow the animal to lead a normal predatory life, if it was to live in the wild. Allowance should be made for sex, i.e. hobs in general are larger than jills. Some clubs' standards favour larger animals, while others favour smaller; it is always worth checking this before entering a show.

Condition, eyes and ears

The ferret should be fit, curious when well awake, and tame to handle. The flesh should be firm with no surplus fat, and the coat have a health sheen, with the ferret being quite clean. The eyes should be small and widely set, with the ears being small and discreet, set well apart on the head. The teeth should be white and the ferret should have a complete set; penalties will be incurred for missing, damaged or rotten teeth. The jaws should meet correctly.

Penalties will be incurred for the following reasons;

> Intractability (i.e. not tame)
> disease or injury
> excess fat
> sores, wounds or scars
> dirty fur
> missing limb, eye, ear, foot or tail
> any deformity believed by the judge to be hereditary
> under/over-shot jaws
> damaged, missing or rotten teeth

No penalties should be incurred by ferrets with a slight amount of wax in their ears. This is perfectly normal, and is actually an aid to the ferret's well-being. However, where the ears have been scrubbed out, and may even show signs of irritation from the process, penalties should be incurred.

To compete successfully over a prolonged period, you must learn about basic genetics and the skills required to practice selective breeding. I suggest you read one of my other books on ferrets - "The Complete Guide to Ferrets" (Swan Hill Press, 1995).

Ferret racing

This sport originated in the USA, and has been taken up with much enthusiasm here in the UK. There are many country fairs and similar events where ferrets are raced for the entertainment of the public. When properly organised, the crowds find the spectacle fascinating, and the ferrets seem to really enjoy themselves.

The start of this sport came about when oil workers were using ferrets to pass lines through the oil pipelines they were laying across the deserts in the US. Once through, the lines could be attached to cameras, welding machinery etc, which could be hauled through the pipe. At night, with very little to do, the workers would take bets on the fastest ferret to go through a length of pipe.

When the idea arrived in the UK, it was suitably tweaked to allow for British conditions. Today, the average ferret race takes place between 4-6 ferrets, who have to run down identical lengths of piping (all of the same bore). At intervals along the pipes, gaps are left (to help the public see where the ferrets are), and the trick is to encourage the ferrets to continue to the end of the piping. Great fun, and a way in which we help raise funds for good causes.

If you want to get involved with showing or racing your ferrets, contact your local club, or attend a country fair or similar event, where most ferret clubs have a "have-a-go" stand for the general public to enter their ferrets.

Young fitchet running

7.

FERRET AILMENTS

Ferrets are healthy animals, provided that the husbandry of the animals is good. If you follow the advice given in this book, you shouldn't go far wrong. However, even the best looked-after animals can still occasionally fall ill. The main problem is that ferrets mask their symptoms, often until the eleventh hour, thus making them difficult to treat. To make life even more complicated, UK vets do not see ferrets as often as they should and in fact need to. The less experience the vets have with a species, the less successful their treatment of that animal is going to be, and the less likely they are to see more of the same species. Thus a steep downward spiral develops, in which the ultimate loser is the ferret. If your ferret is sick, take it to your local veterinary surgeon, in exactly the same way that you would ensure your pet dog receives the appropriate treatment.

I have listed some of the main ailments that your ferret may suffer from, and these are arranged in alphabetical order. Be aware that similar symptoms exist for entirely different illnesses. This section is intended as a guide for the ferret owner, but it is always best to have a qualified veterinary surgeon check out any sick or ailing animal as soon as practical.

ALEUTIAN DISEASE (AD)

Aleutian disease (AD) is caused by a parvovirus and is an immune deficiency disease, capable of being transmitted from infected parents to offspring and from infected ferrets to any other ferret via direct or indirect contact. Symptoms vary tremendously and may include black tarry faeces, weight loss, aggressiveness, recurrent fevers, thyroiditis, posterior paralysis, and eventual death; in stressed animals, death may occur extremely suddenly. Veterinary advice should be sought for all ferrets thought to be infected, or in contact with an infected ferret.

ACTINOMYCOSIS

An acute hard swelling of the ferret's neck, actinomycosis is probably caused by abrasions to the animal's oesophagus, usually by feeding too many day-old chicks in the diet. Affected ferrets will be listless, anorexic and have a fever. Refer the animal to a vet without delay.

BOTULISM

Botulism is a killer, and is caused by one of the most common bacterium known to science, Clostridium botulinum, a natural contaminant of most wild bird cadavers. When this bacterium comes into contact with any decaying flesh (ie meat), it causes a deadly toxin to be formed. If this flesh is then eaten by an animal, the toxin affects its victim by attacking the animal's nervous system, causing paralysis, at first usually in the hind legs, eventually affecting the body's vital organs, and leads inevitably to the death of the affected animal. There is no cure or treatment for this, and ferrets are among the most susceptible animals to botulism.

DIARRHOEA

Diarrhoea is a symptom and NOT a disease; it is indicative of a problem, which may be serious or minor, but will still require investigation. In ferrets, this condition is often referred to as the 'scours', and is often a sign that the animal has been fed on a poor diet, or its food is contaminated. Diarrhoea can also be indicative of some other, more serious affliction, such as poisoning, internal parasites or even stress. You should isolate the affected ferret(s) and seek veterinary advice immediately.

DISTEMPER (CANINE DISTEMPER) (CD)

Ferrets are highly susceptible to canine distemper, a virus which is one of the most common fatal diseases in ferrets; dogs are the most common source of such an infection. If you take your ferret into areas where unvaccinated dogs may have been, you should have all of your ferrets vaccinated against this disease as a matter of course. Symptoms of CD are swollen feet, leading to hard pad, the actual thickening of the soles of the feet and a classical sign of distemper infection, runny eyes and nose, diarrhoea, lack of appetite, a larger than average thirst and a rash, usually under the chin. In its latter stages, the infected animal will vomit, have convulsions and, shortly before dying, will pass into a coma. This disease is highly contagious and, at the first signs of distemper, all infected ferrets must be isolated. Immediate veterinary advice must be sought.

ENTERITIS

Enteritis is an inflammation of the intestines, causing diarrhoea, and is very common among kits and young stock. Immediate treatment with a broad spectrum antibiotic, supplemented with regular doses of kaolin, may cure this condition. If left untreated, the affected animal will most definitely die.

HEATSTROKE (THE 'SWEATS')

Ferrets cannot tolerate high temperatures, reacting adversely to too much heat, and may well die from heatstroke, often referred to as "the sweats". This is a rather misleading term since ferrets cannot sweat. The first sign of heatstroke or heat exhaustion is an agitated ferret in obvious distress. If left untreated, they will eventually collapse, pass into a coma and die. In all cases, it is vital to keep the head cool, as brain death can occur, as the brain is quite literally 'pickled'. Veterinary advice should be sought at the earliest opportunity.

HYPOCALCAEMIA

A lack of calcium in the blood, this affliction can occur 3 - 4 weeks after the jill has given birth. Posterior paralysis and convulsions are common symptoms, while the cause is usually a poor diet. Feeding a diet heavily dependent on day-old chicks will almost certainly lead to this complaint. Consult your veterinary surgeon immediately; after treatment a calcium rich diet is essential for total recovery.

INFLUENZA

Ferrets can catch influenza, ("the 'flu") from their owners, or vice versa. Symptoms in ferrets are the same as in humans - fever, sneezing, lack of appetite, listlessness, runny eyes and a nasal discharge. In adult ferrets, the condition is not usually serious, with most ferrets making a spontaneous recovery, although antibiotics may be necessary to control some secondary infections. Influenza is, however, almost always fatal in young ferrets. Infected ferrets must be isolated to prevent spread of this condition, and veterinary advice sought.

MANGE

Sarcoptes scabiei causes two types of mange in ferrets, which can become infected through coming into direct contact with other infected animals, such as rodents, or simply by being on infected ground. One type of mange causes alopecia and pruritus (an intense itching), while the other causes only foot or toe problems ("foot rot"). The first sign of mange is persistent scratching, even though there is no obvious cause such as fleas. Eventually, the skin will become very red and sore, a symptom that is easier to notice in albino ferrets than in ones with polecat coloration. As the disease progresses, these sores cause baldness and the sores become even worse. A parasiticidal wash (e.g. bromocyclen) must be applied to the affected areas, or injections of ivermectin administered; this drug cannot be used in the first month of pregnancy, or it will cause congenital defects. Be warned - mange can be contracted by humans, when it is known as scabies.

OESTROGEN-INDUCED ANAEMIA

When a jill is not mated, the levels of oestrogen in her body rise and can have serious effects on the health of the ferret. This frequently causes progressive depression of the bone marrow, often resulting in a condition known as pancytopoenia - the abnormal depression of all three elements of blood - which is debilitating and potentially fatal. Signs include weight loss, alopecia, anorexia, pale lips and gums, difficulty in breathing and, in later stages, darkening of faeces (caused by blood), and bleeding sores on the animal's flanks and abdomen. There may also be secondary infections. In its advanced stages, treatment is highly unlikely to be effective. In early stages, spaying or hormonal treatment to stop oestrus with repeated transfusions of fresh whole blood containing 1 ml of sodium citrate can be used effectively.

OSTEODYSTROPHY

Defective bone formations, often due to hyperphosphorosis (too much phosphorous in the diet) is caused by feeding a diet consisting entirely of, or rich in, muscle meat; this lacks calcium, and leads to a deficiency of this vital mineral. The problem usually manifests itself in young ferrets (6 - 12 weeks), who have difficulty walking, moving instead with the gait of a seal, with the legs (particularly the front legs) sticking out to the side of the body rather than pointing to the floor; death is common. Veterinary advice must be sought when ferrets have difficulty walking in a normal manner.

PARASITES

Ferrets can suffer from the unwanted attentions of either internal (endoparasites) or external (ectoparasites) parasites. Ferrets can suffer from worms, Toxocara or Toxascaris, but these are not usually problematical. (However they can be dangerous to human beings if they are ingested or touched.) A vet will prescribe an anthelmintic (an agent which is destructive to worms) such as mebendazole or fenbenzadole. Heart worms, coccidia, Toxiplasma, and Pneumocystis are sometimes found. Veterinary examination and clinical investigation of the faeces will be necessary to positively identify the actual problem. The first sign of a worm infestation is an insatiable appetite coupled with a steady loss of weight. Sometimes, segments of the worms may be found in the ferret's faeces before other symptoms indicate a problem.

FLEAS

Ctenocephalides, and ticks - Ixodes ricinus, are external parasites that most ferrets will catch at some stage, especially if used for hunting. These ectoparasites are contracted from animals such as dogs, cats, rabbits and other such species. Insecticidal preparations intended for dogs and cats are safe to use on ferrets. With new preparations coming on to the market all the time, care must always be taken to ensure that any product is safe before you use it on your ferrets. Do not forget that you will have to adjust the dosage to suit the size of the ferret, as per the manufacturer's instructions.

TICKS

Ticks are rather more difficult to deal with than fleas, but they do respond to some sprays and powders, although these may only be available from veterinary surgeons. Care must be taken to ensure that the mouth parts of ticks are completely removed from the ferret's skin, otherwise infection and abscesses can occur; never simply pull ticks out. Paint surgical spirit on the tick using a fine paint brush, and the tick should have died and dropped off within 24 hours; if not, simply repeat the process. Although some authorities suggest that ticks be burned off with a lighted cigarette, this should never be attempted. It is all too easy to burn the ferret with the cigarette and the alcohol method is much more effective, with none of the dangers. There are now a number of devices on the market which have been specifically designed to remove ticks, due mainly to concern regarding Lyme's disease in humans, and these are recommended.

Fleas on ferret kits.
Fleas also bite humans!

POSTERIOR PARALYSIS ("THE STAGGERS")

The causes of paralysis in ferrets are many and varied, including disease of the spinal disks, hypocalcaemia (lack of calcium in the blood), Aleutian disease, viral myelitis (inflammation of the spinal cord), cancer of the spine, vertebral trauma, or even a dietary deficiency. It is often caused by injury, and paralysis can also be inherited. In all cases of paralysis, veterinary advice must be sought immediately.

PYOMETRA

This is the accumulation of pus within the uterus, and is only occasionally seen in ferrets. When it does occur, it is immediately after the start of a pseudo-pregnancy. Organisms responsible for this condition in ferrets include Streptococcus, Staphylococcus, E. coli, Corynebacterium. Affected ferrets will be anorexic, lethargic, and will often have a fever. Medical attention must be sought immediately, as the uterus may rupture.

SKIN TUMOURS (NEOPLASIA)

These are unfortunately common in ferrets. In all cases surgery is necessary and should be carried out as soon as possible. These tumours are however very difficult to eliminate and frequently recur. Warts also occur on ferrets, and so it is vital that histopathology is used to confirm all diagnoses. Consult your vet if any animal develops lumps anywhere on its body.

THIAMINE DEFICIENCY

Where ferrets are fed a diet consisting of a large proportion of day-old chicks, raw fish or eggs (or a combination of any or all of these items), a thiamine deficiency is almost guaranteed. Symptoms include anorexia, lethargy, weakness of the hindquarters and convulsions. All cases of convulsions, paralysis or unusual behaviour should be referred to your vet.

TUBERCULOSIS

Ferrets are susceptible to avian, bovine and human tuberculosis, with symptoms which include paralysis of the limbs, diarrhoea and wasting of the body. Almost always fatal, the disease is highly contagious; contact your vet at once if you suspect this condition in your ferrets.

ZINC TOXICITY

Ferrets cannot tolerate high levels of zinc, and may become ill through the use of galvanised feeding dishes. Symptoms include anaemia, lethargy and weakness of the hind legs; liver and kidney failure can quickly follow, so all suspected cases should be referred to a vet as soon as possible. Unfortunately there is no actual treatment and affected animals are unlikely to recover. It is common for vets to advise euthanasia for affected ferrets to avoid undue suffering.

Three young fitchets

Albino ferret kits
8-10 weeks old

8.

FIRST AID FOR FERRETS

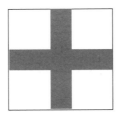

The principles of first aid

All first aid principles are the same, regardless of species involved, and we cannot recommend too highly that everyone should have a basic training in the subject. At the National Ferret School we run courses on ferret first aid, while organisations such as the Red Cross and the St. John's Ambulance Service run courses on human first aid. Attending one may help you save a life - human or ferret.

The old saying that things are as easy as A B C is very true when it comes to first aid:

Airways

Breathing

Circulation

In other words, if the patient is not breathing, get the airways clear before you try to get the ferret breathing, and only once they are breathing should you concern yourself with the heart and/or bleeding.

The objectives of first aid are three fold - to sustain life, to prevent the patient's condition worsening, and to promote recovery. The methods used are;

1. Assess the situation

2. Diagnose the condition

3. Treat immediately and adequately

Remember to ensure your own safety at all times.

A first aid kit for ferrets

A suitable first aid kit should contain the following items as a minimum. They should always accompany you on any field trip and be near at hand at all times.

Styptic pencil	**Tweezers**
Scissors	**Adhesive plasters**
Surgical gauze	**Bandages**
Table salt	**Sodium Bicarbonate**
Cotton wool	**Antihistamine**
Cotton buds	**Antiseptic powder**
Antiseptic lotion	**Surgical spirits**

INSECT BITES (INCLUDING STINGS)

Clip a little fur away from the area, so that you can actually see the problem, then wash with saline solution. Bees leave their sting in the victim, wasps do not. If there is a sting present, it should be carefully removed with the tweezers and then the area wiped with cotton wool (or a cotton bud) soaked in alcohol, such as surgical spirits. For wasp stings, a little vinegar will prove beneficial, while for bee stings, use a little bicarbonate of soda. Dry the area thoroughly, and use an antihistamine spray or apply a wet compress to help reduce the irritation and swelling. If the ferret has been bitten or stung in the throat, veterinary attention must be sought as soon as possible; such stings can cause swelling that may block the airways and thus kill the ferret.

FERRET BITES

Although it may at first seem strange, ferrets are more likely to suffer from bites from other ferrets than from any other animal. This is specially true during the breeding season, when the hob takes hold of the jill by the scruff, hanging on tightly and very often breaking the jill's skin with his teeth. These types of injuries are not usually serious, providing that they are given first aid treatment as soon as possible. The area of the bite must be clipped of fur, and the wound thoroughly washed with a saline solution followed by an antiseptic liquid. A good dusting with wound powder will finish the job. If action is not taken, the wound may fester and result in abscesses. If the wound is serious, veterinary treatment should be sought.

BREATHING PROBLEMS

Ferrets gasping for breath are obviously showing symptoms of some form of breathing difficulty; this may be heatstroke ("the sweats'), fluid on the lungs or an obstruction of some kind. Many obstructions can be removed from a ferret's mouth with a cotton bud or even a finger. Artificial respiration, though difficult, is possible with ferrets. If a ferret has stopped breathing, rather than give mouth-to-mouth respiration, hold the ferret by its hind legs and, keeping your arms straight, swing the animal to the left and then to the right. This transfers the weight of the ferret's internal organs on and off the diaphragm, causing the lungs to fill and empty of air. Keep this up until the ferret begins breathing on its own, help arrives, or you believe the ferret to be beyond help.

CONVULSIONS

Convulsions are a symptom, an indication that the ferret has an infection of some kind or has been poisoned, and NOT a disease. There are obviously many possible causes for convulsions, and one of the most common in captive ferrets is heatstroke, or the 'sweats'. However, if your ferret is suffering from convulsions, you should seek urgent medical attention for the ailing animal.

INCISED (CLEAN) CUT

These are straight cuts, as one would get from a sharp knife blade; as such, they bleed profusely. This bleeding can be very frightening to people not used to such things - a little blood appears as "gallons" to most lay people, even though there may only be a thimble full! In fact, bleeding helps to clean the wound of debris, and this lessens the possibility of infection. Bleeding should be stemmed by direct pressure, if at all possible. Where it is not, apply indirect pressure on an artery at the heart side of the wound. Elevating the injury will enable gravity to help reduce the blood flow. Apply a suitable dressing; large and/or deep cuts will almost certainly require sutures (stitches) from a qualified vet.

LACERATED CUTS

These are tears in the skin, as caused by barbed wire, for instance, and will bleed less profusely than incised cuts. The big danger is that the injury will have pushed dirt and debris into the wound, and the lack of bleeding will mean that the dirt is not washed out. You must clean the wound with a saline solution (salt water - 1 teaspoonful to one litre of warm water); dry it and apply a dressing if necessary.

CONTUSION (BRUISE)

This is a sign of internal bleeding, and a careful watch must be kept on the injured animal. If shock sets in, seek veterinary advice immediately.

PUNCTURE (STAB)

Puncture wounds, which can be caused by nails, slivers of wood and other such objects, usually appear very small at the surface but, of course, could be very deep. NEVER remove any object from a wound, as this may aggravate the injury and/or allow large amounts of bleeding. Apply pressure around the wound site, using a dressing to maintain the pressure, and seek medical attention immediately.

FRACTURES

Fractures are caused by either direct or indirect pressure on the bones, which may crack or actually break. Where the bone is broken and pierces the skin, this is known as an open or compound fracture, and all others as closed fractures. Signs of such injury are obvious - painful movement of the limb, tenderness, swelling, loss of control of the limb, deformity of the limb, unnatural movement of the limb, and crepitus (the sensation or, in very bad cases, the sound of the two ends of the bones grinding on each other). Keep the patient quiet, and steady and support the injured limb, immobilising it with bandages and splints if necessary, to prevent it moving and causing greater damage. Raising the limb will help reduce discomfort and swelling (by reducing the blood flow).

HEATSTROKE (THE 'SWEATS')

Ferrets cannot tolerate high temperatures, reacting adversely to too much heat, and may well die from heatstroke, often referred to as "the sweats", a rather misleading term since ferrets cannot sweat. Of course, prevention is better than cure and the siting of the cage is very important, as is the position that they are left in while out working. In the confines of a carrying box or even a motor car, the temperature can quickly rise to a dangerous level, even in the cooler sunshine of autumn and spring.

No animals should be left unattended in a vehicle, or transported in such a manner that they or their carrying box are in full sunlight. The sun does not stay in the same position throughout the day, and even if the box or car is in the shadows when you leave it, it may not stay that way for long. When you return, to your car, your ferrets may well be dead.

In extreme summer temperatures, or in areas where it is known that temperature will be high, every effort must be made to insulate the cage, and place it in an area where it and its inmates are protected from the full effect of varying temperatures. Where it is not possible to keep the ferrets' cage as cool as one would like, wet cloths may be hung over the cage to keep the temperature down, although they will soon dry out, and so require constant attention throughout the day. Placing bricks on each corner of the cage roof, and then positioning a piece of timber over them, will act as "double glazing", and will be extremely effective in reducing heat build-up in the cage.

The first sign of heatstroke or heat exhaustion is an agitated ferret in obvious distress. If in their cage, affected ferrets will stretch out and pant heavily. If left untreated, they will eventually collapse, pass into a coma and die. Immediately a ferret shows symptoms of heatstroke, you must act - and fast; delay can be fatal. The ferret's body is over-heating, and so your first task must be to lower its body temperature. With mildly affected ferrets, simply moving them to a cool area, and ensuring a steady passage of cool air over them, is usually effective; a light spraying with cold water from a plant mister is beneficial. In bad cases, where it is literally make or break, the best method is to immerses the animal to the neck in a bucket of cold water, repeating this procedure regularly for the next few minutes, by which time the ferret should be showing signs of recovery.

Ensure that the ferret is thoroughly dried, and placed in a cage in a cool area, with a small towel for bedding; this will also help to dry the ferret's coat.

This is a very drastic "treatment", and should only be attempted where the animal is very badly affected. In all cases, it is vital to keep the head cool, as brain death can occur, as the brain is quite literally 'pickled'. Veterinary advice should be sought at the earliest opportunity.

....

If in any doubt about the health of your ferret - seek the advice of a qualified veterinary surgeon as soon as possible.

Appendix A: Glossary of ferret terms

ALBINO. A white ferret, with no pigmentation in its flesh or eyes. The eyes are opaque but, due to the fact that blood can be seen behind the eyes, they appear pink. There are several other types of white ferrets which are NOT albinos.

BENCHING. The act of placing ferrets on the show bench, for the attention of the judge officiating at that show.

BUSINESS. The collective term for a group of ferrets.

CAGE. The container in which ferrets are kept. These can be commercially manufactured or home made by breeders using wood, plastic or metal. See also "Court" and "Cub".

CANINES. The front teeth of a ferret which it uses to kill its prey.

CLASSES. At a ferret show, entries are divided in to classes, to facilitate judging. These classes are usually dictated by the colour, variety or sex of the ferret concerned.

COURT. A traditional type of cage, rather like a birds' aviary, in which ferrets are kept.

CUB. The traditional name for the hutch-like cage in which some ferrets are kept.

FERRET. The domesticated European polecat (*Mustella putorius*). The term is often (erroneously) used to describe only the albino version of this species.

FITCH. The ferret's fur.

FITCHET. A polecat-coloured ferret.

HEAT. The state in which a jill will accept a mating. See also "oestrus"

HOB. A male ferret or polecat.

HOBBLE. A castrated hob.

HOBLET. A vasectomised hob.

INTRACTABILITY. Lack of tameness, being impossible to handle without the risk of being bitten.

JILL. A female ferret or polecat.

KIT. A young ferret, usually used to describe a ferret of sixteen weeks of age or less. Comes from the name of the young of the polecat i.e. pole-kitten!

MASK. The markings on the face of a polecat (or polecat ferret or fitchet). This mask is usually darker in the summer than in the winter.

MUSK. The foul smelling scent produced by the anal glands of ferrets and polecats.

OESTRUS. The state in which a jill will accept a mating. See also 'Heat'.

OESTRUS CYCLE. The sexual cycle of a female ferret.

PHOTOPERIODISM. The dependence on the daytime/night-time (or simply light and dark) ratio of various biological functions, particularly the commencement of oestrus.

POLECAT. The common name of the animal *Mustela putorius*. Strictly, this name should only be used to describe the wild polecat, but today it is also commonly used to describe any domesticated ferret with polecat type markings. The name originates from the French "Poule Chat" - chicken cat!

POLEY. A domesticated ferret with the typical wild polecat markings, i.e. a fitchet

QUIET. The term used to describe a ferret which is easy to handle.

SANDY. A coloured ferret with colouring between an albino and a polecat.

SCOURS. Diarrhoea

SEXUAL DIMORPHISM. The differences exhibited between the sexes e.g. the male ferret always has the capacity to grow larger than the female (up to twice the size).

SIBLING. Brother or sister; litter mate.

SWEATS. Overheating

VARIETY. A specific colour and coat type of the ferret, e.g. albino.

WEANING. The development of the eating habits of ferret kits when they progress from being dependent upon their mothers for food, and are capable of feeding themselves, i.e. eating solid food.

ZOONOSES. Diseases capable of being transmitted from an animal to a human e.g. salmonellosis.

Appendix B: Ferret facts & figures

THE ADULT FERRET

Average weight (adult)	Between 400gm and 2 kg. Hobs weigh up to twice as much as jills.
Average size (adult)	Between 35 and 60 cm (hob up to twice size of jill)
Average lifespan	Between 8 and 12 years (in captivity)
Rectal temperature	38.6 degrees Centigrade (Range 37.8 - 40.0)
Heart Rate	220 - 250 b.p.m.
Respiratory rate	30 - 40 per minute
Number of toes	5 per foot
Teeth	Incisors 3/3, canines 1/1, premolars 3/3, molars 1/2.
Nipples	2 rows of 4 (8 in total) - on both sexes
Sexing	Ano-genital distance of female half that of male
No. of chromosomes	40 (20 pairs)

Fitchets

BREEDING

Normal breeding season Early March to late September (Britain).

Breeding Season   Triggered by photoperiod - longer days than nights.

First possible mating 6 months i.e. first spring after birth.

Duration of oestrus   Ceases when mated; if unmated, will continue to
                       end of 'season', often causing medical problems.

Signs of Oestrus   Vulva swells, becomes vivid pink colour, secretion.

                       In male, testes swell and descend into scrotum.

Duration of oestrus   Until mated or end of spring/summer (can last for
                       up to 6 months).

Duration of mating   Several hours.

Kit
3 weeks old

PREGNANCY

Ovulation	About 30 hours after coitus.
Reduction of vulva	Begins 7 - 10 days after mating, complete within 2 - 3 weeks.
Palpation	10 days after vulva totally reduced.
Gestation (pregnancy)	40 - 44 days; average 42 days.
Number of young	1 - 15 (average 6 - 8). Jills can have up to two litters per year.
	Largest litter ever recorded - 19.
Litters per year	1 or 2.
Post natal oestrus	1 - 2 weeks after weaning.

Baby polecat ferrets
3 weeks old

KIT DEVELOPMENT

Weight at birth — 5 - 15gm.

State at birth — Blind, deaf, naked and entirely dependent upon the mother.

Ears/eyes open — 22 - 36 days.

Fur — In dark coloured kits, starts to appear within 5 - 7 days. Good covering by 4 weeks.

Deciduous teeth — Erupt at 10 - 14 days.

Movement — Kits as young as 2 - 3 weeks will manage to crawl out of nest (to be dragged back by the mother).

Canine teeth — 47 - 52 days.

Weaning — 7 - 9 weeks.

Weight at weaning — 300 - 500 g.

Age attain adult weight — 4 - 5 months.

Age at puberty — About 8 months or 250 days.

Age at sexual maturity — 6 to 12 months (spring after birth).

Two fitchets
curled up together

Appendix C: Useful books

The inclusion of a title does not infer any endorsement by the author; neither does the omission of a title infer lack of approval.

Biology and Diseases of the Ferret
James G Fox
Publishers - Lea & Febiger (1988)

The Complete Book of Ferrets
Val Porter and Nicholas Brown
Publishers - Pelham Books (1985)

Colour Inheritance in Small Livestock
Roy Robinson
Publishers - Fur & Feather (1978)

The Ferret and Ferreting Guide
Graham Welstead
Publishers - David and Charles (1981)

The Ferret & Ferreting Handbook
James McKay
Publishers - The Crowood Press (1989)

Ferrets
Jay & Mary Field
Publishers - TFH (1987)

Complete Guide to Ferrets
James McKay
Publishers Swan Hill Press (1995)

Ferrets
Wendy Winstead
Publishers - TFH (1981)

Modern Ferreting
Brian Plummer
Publishers - Boydell Press (1977)

Guide to Ferreting
Fred J Taylor
Publishers - Buchan & Enright (1983)

Ferrets - A Complete Pet Owner's Manual
Chuck and Fox Morton
Publishers - Barron's (1985)

Stoats & Weasels, Polecats & Martens
Paddy Sleeman
Publishers - Whittet Books (1989)

Appendix D: Useful addresses

Please note: The following were all correct at then time of going to press; however, details and officers do change, especially where the organisation is a voluntary one. In all cases, where a reply is required, always enclose a self-addressed and stamped envelope with all enquiries. The inclusion of an organisation does not imply any standard or the author's approval of that organisation; neither does the exclusion of any organisations imply any disapproval.

The East Anglian Ferret Welfare Association
35 Lamborne Gardens
Hornchurch, Essex RM12 4LJ

The Essex Ferret Welfare Society
21 Moreton Road
Shelley, Ongar, Essex CM5 0AP

The Gem Ferret Care Group
24 Arden Road, Furnace Green
Crawley, West Sussex RH10 6HS

The Kent Ferret Welfare Society
5 Eastern Gardens
Willesborough, Ashford
Kent TN24 0HE

The South East Ferret Club
Westbury 2, Waterditch Road
Warren Street, Lenham
Kent ME17 2DY

South Yorkshire Ferrets
57 Adkins Road,
Sheffield S5 8TF

Deben Group Industries
Deben Way
Melton, Woodbridge,
Suffolk IP12 1RB

Manufacturers of ferret detectors and other electronic equipment.

James Wellbeloved & Co Ltd
25 Brympton Way
Yeovil, Somerset BA20 2JB
Tel: 01935-410600

Makers of Ferret Complete, the complete and balanced dry ferret food. The company also produces top quality dry dog and cat foods.

The National Database of Ferret Friendly Vets
PO Box 61
Chesterfield
Derbyshire S45 0YU

This is a computer data base of veterinary surgeons, established by the author, who have experience or interest in ferrets and their ailments. Addition to the database is free, and responses to enquiries are also free providing a self-addressed and suitably stamped envelope is sent.

The National Ferret School and The Ferret Roadshow
PO Box 61
Chesterfield
Derbyshire S45 0YU

This organisation, of which the author is founder, runs courses on all aspects of ferrets, ferreting, hawking, hawks, owls, falconry etc. Fact and information sheets are also issued by the School, which issued a Code of Conduct for Organisers of Ferret Racing and Displays. The School also sells ferret and ferreting equipment. Please send a large self-addressed and stamped envelope with all enquiries, stating full details of your requirements or enquiry.

Formed by the author in 1982, the Ferret Roadshow travels the UK giving displays and lectures on all aspects of ferrets and ferreting.

Please note: While these details were correct at the time of printing, especially in the case of voluntary or informal centres, some of these organisations may move or close down. We cannot guarantee that all the above will be available for the future.

Appendix E: Rescue & advice centres

International Ferret Welfare
Show, rescue and advice
Chris and Helga
01922-627029

Independent Ferreters
Rescue and advice
Mike Harris
01753-711818

Sussex Ferret Welfare
Ferret displays, rescue and advice
Roger Sked
01730-814948

Cumbria Ferret Welfare
Rescue and advice. Shows
Marjorie & Alan Thompson
01931-712654

Anjavek Ferrets
Rehoming and advice
Trevor & Karen Smith
01604-466011

Liverpool Ferret Welfare
Betty Shepherd
0151-4804211

Southdown Ferret Fanciers
Carol Welch
01903-521869

Please note: While these details were correct at the time of printing, especially in the case of voluntary or informal centres, some of these organisations may move or close down. We cannot guarantee that all the above will be available for the future.